This Book Belongs to:

_____

BIG

LITTLE

COLD

THIRSTY

TIRED

APPLE

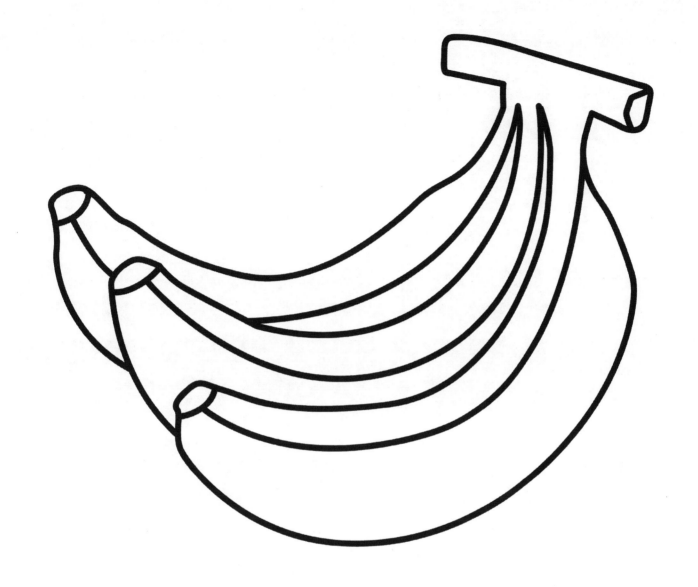

BANANA

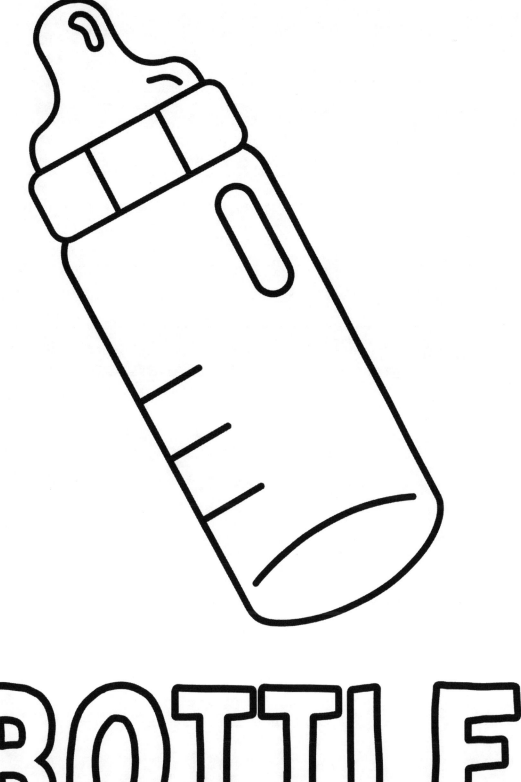

BOTTLE

CHEESE

COOKIE

CRACKER

JUICE

MILK

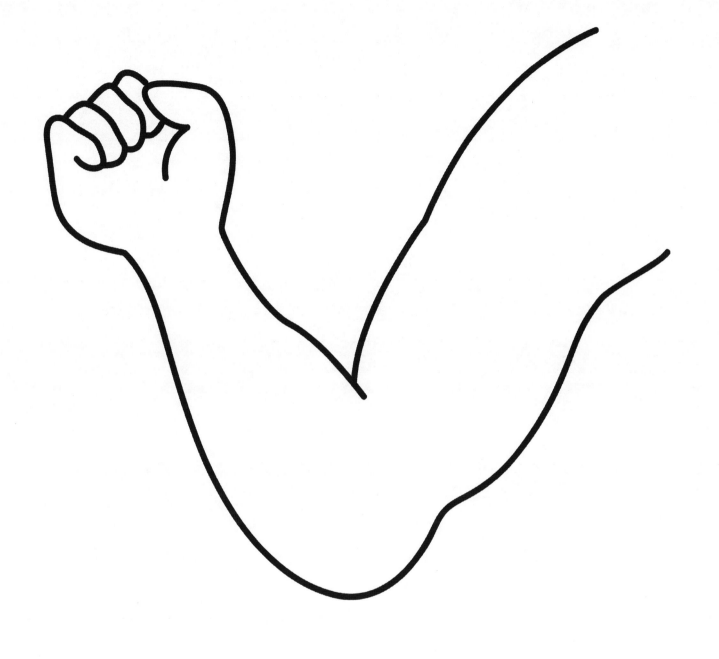

ARM

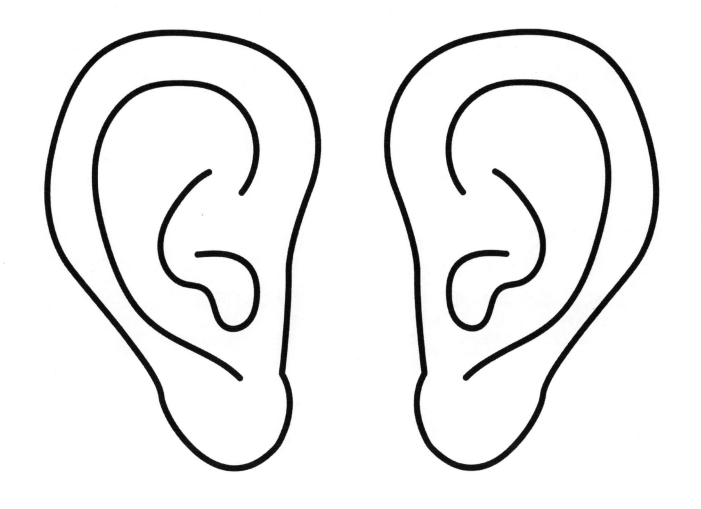

EARS

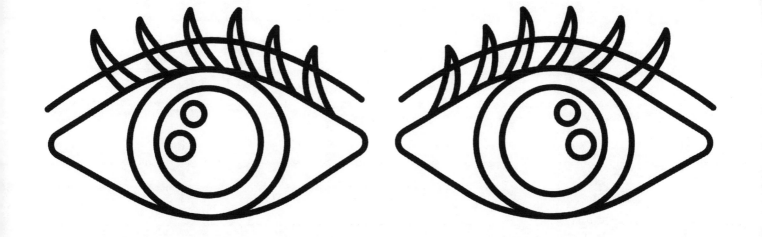

EYES

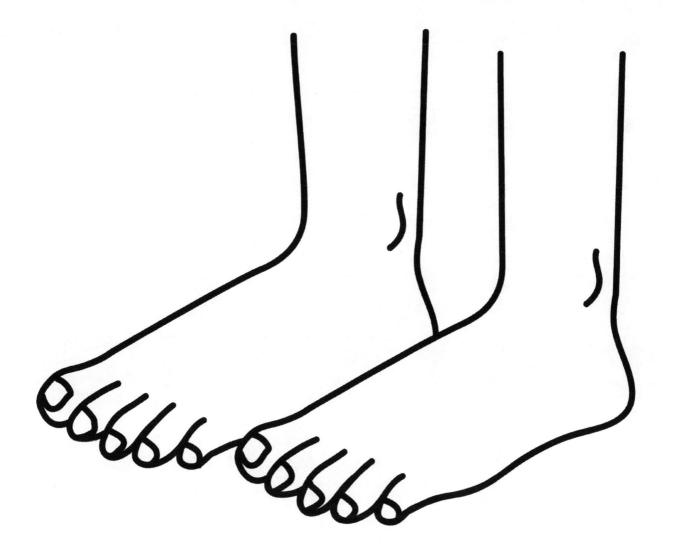

FEET

HANDS

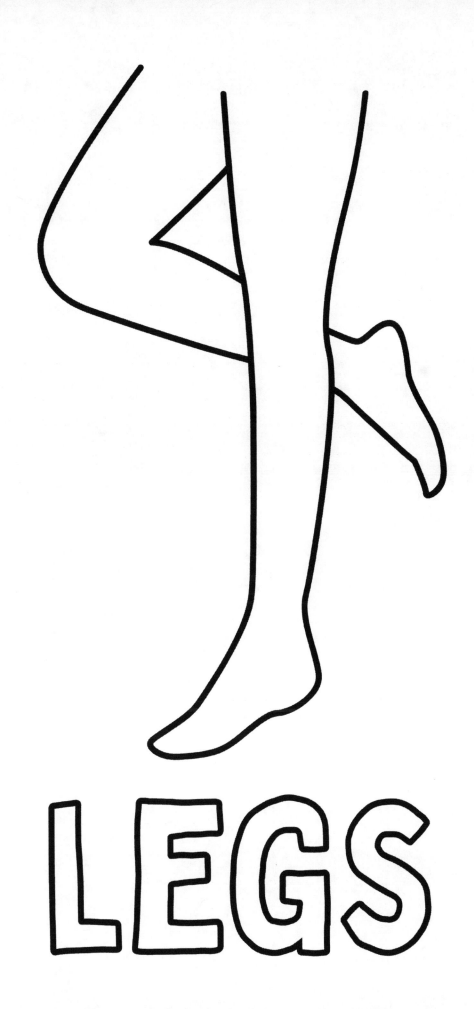

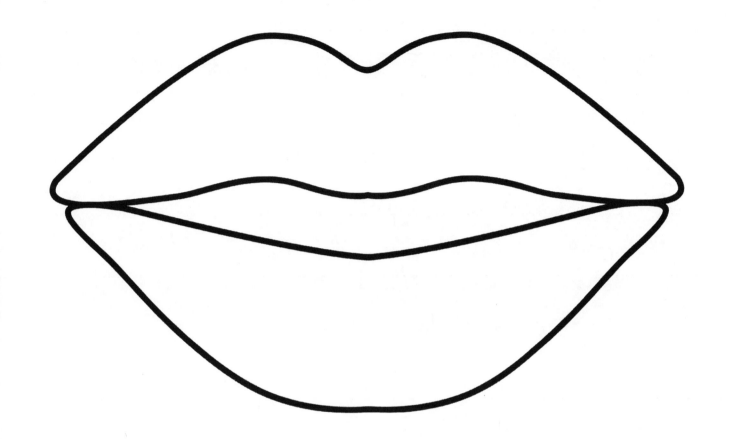

MOUTH

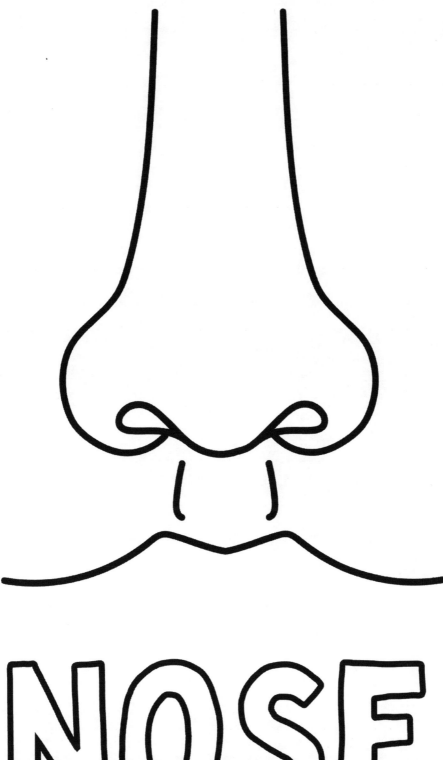

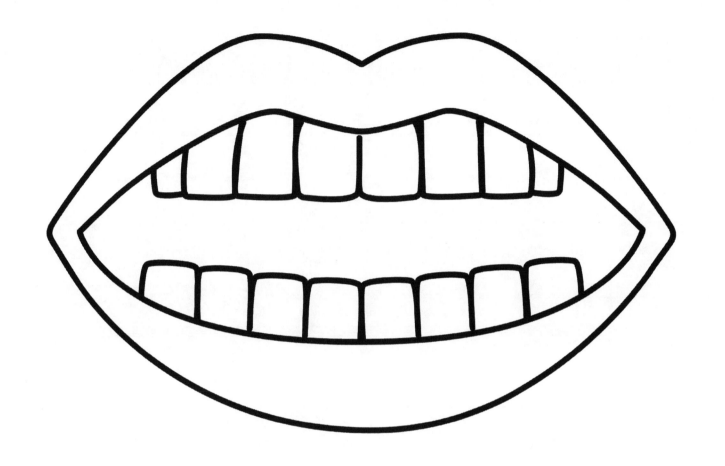

TEETH

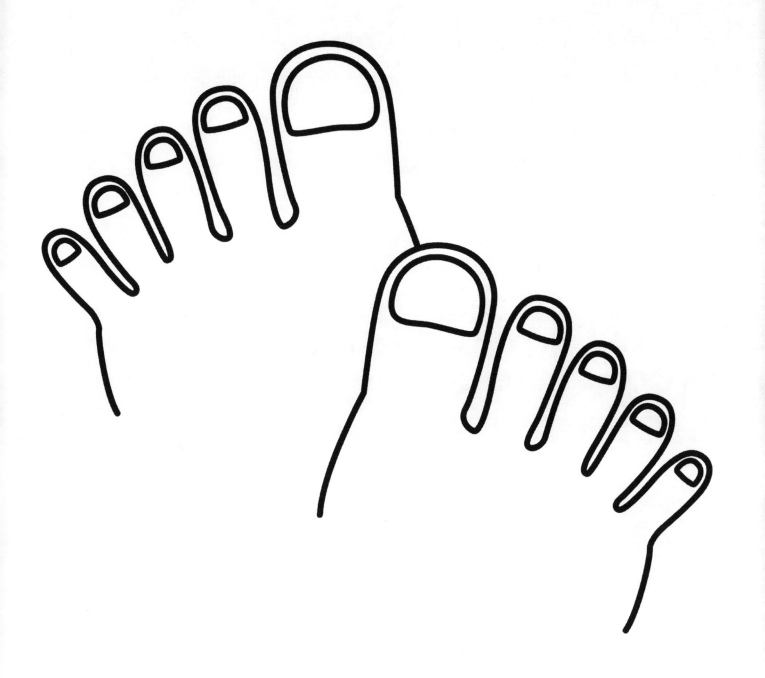

PANTS

SHOES

EAT

DRINK

JUMP

SLEEP

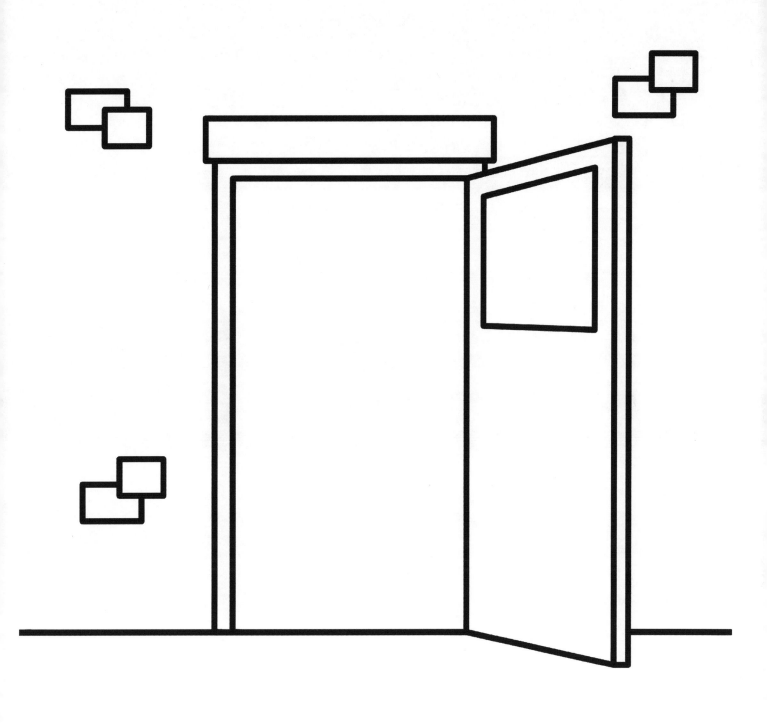

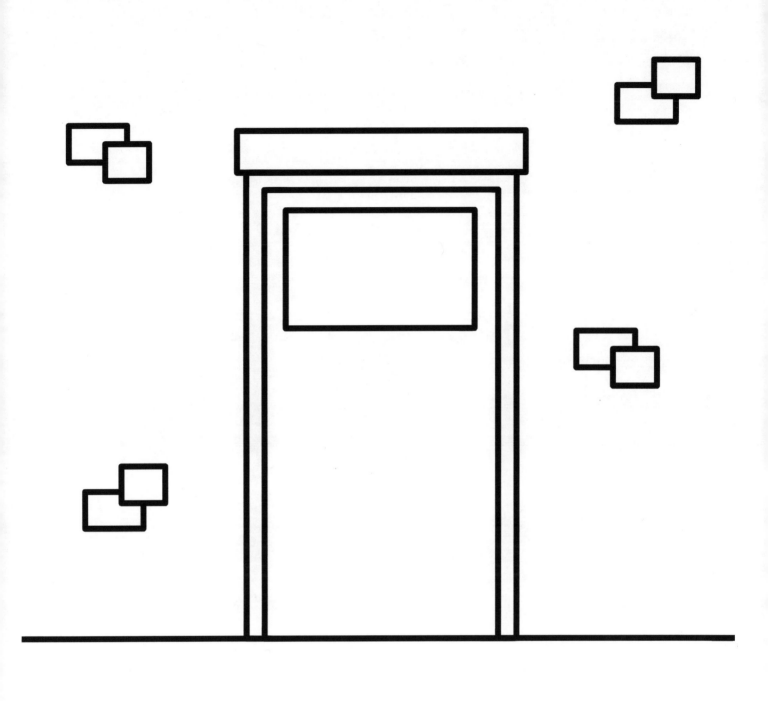

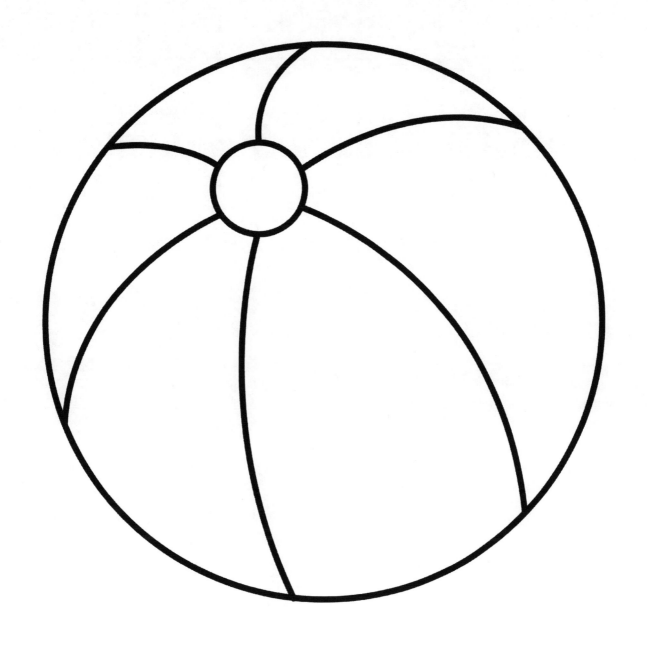

BALL

BATH

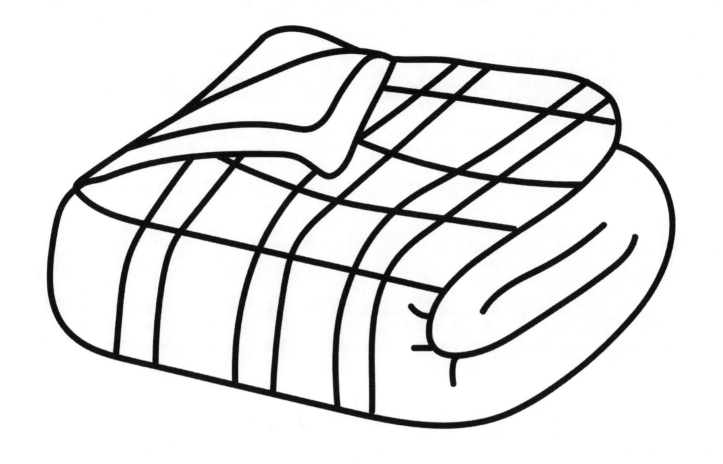

BLANKET

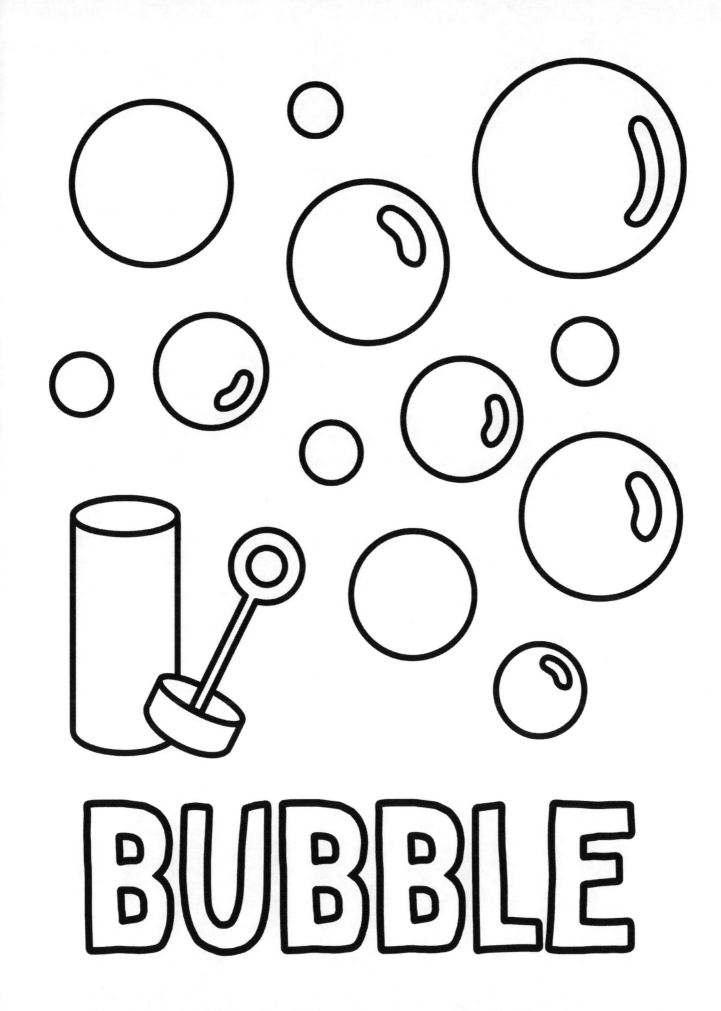

BED

BIKE

BOOK

BUS

CAR

PAPER

PHONE

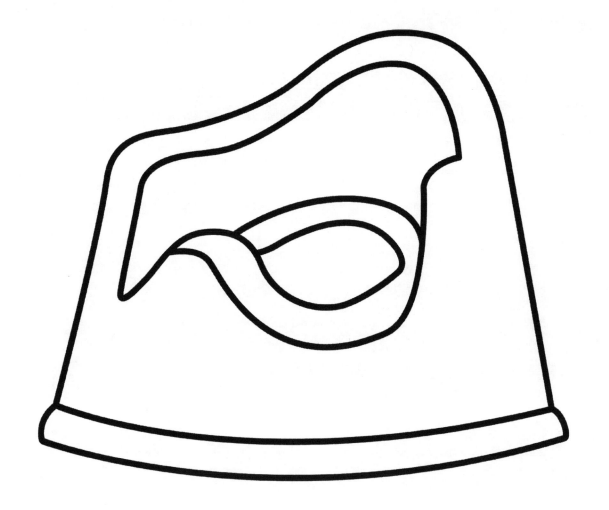

POTTY

TOY

TRAIN

TRUCK

BEE

FISH

FLOWER

GRASS

SLIDE

ROCK

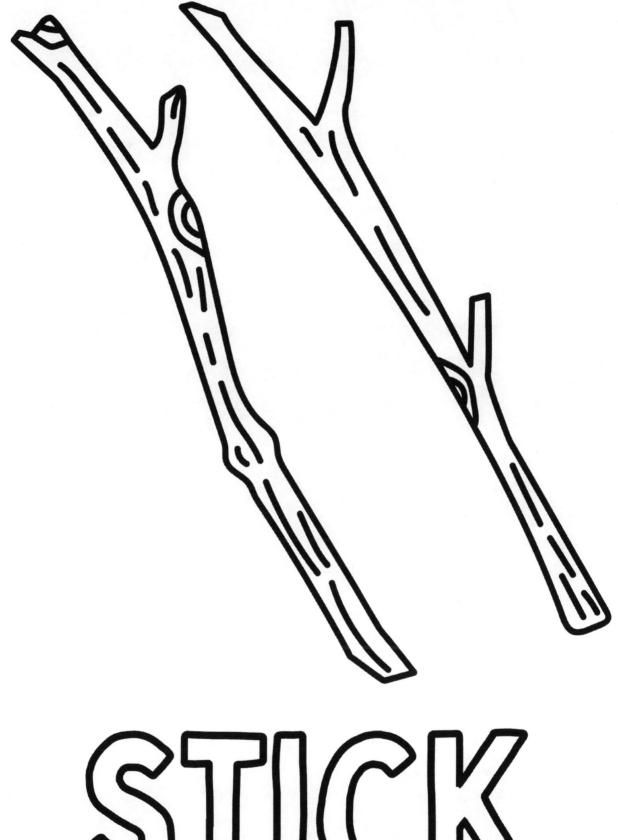

STICK

Please consider leaving a review of our book on Amazon.
We'd appreciate it very much!

Thank you!
The happy crayons team

And if you're looking for more to color, please visit:
happycrayons.com

Copyright © 2022 by Simple Future LLC.
All rights reserved.

ISBN: 978-1-7368948-8-0

No part of this publication may be reproduced, distributed, or transmitted in any form or by any means, including photocopying, recording, or other electronic or mechanical methods, without the prior written permission of the publisher, except in the case of brief quotations for the purposes of book reviews.